I0818934

PUBLISHER'S NOTE TO THE READER.

THE present condition of the country being such as to render important to the people at large the impartial and temperate discussion of sound political principles, in their application to the living issues of the day, I deem the letter of the Hon. Elijah Ward to the New-York *World* well worthy of publication in a more permanent form.

F. B. PATTERSON.

THE

PRINCIPLES AND POLICY

OF

THE DEMOCRATIC PARTY.

In the present state of the nation, it is of the highest importance that correct views and principles should be placed before the people, thus contributing to the progress of sound opinion. A candid exposition of the perils surrounding us is much more conducive to the public interests than specious and delusive promises can be. The people are disposed to look to the Democratic party for a return to economy and integrity in the administration of public affairs, and for the introduction and adoption of measures well calculated to restore to a safe and harmonious basis the financial, commercial, and material interests of the nation. It yet remains to be seen whether the future leaders will fully recognize the exigencies of the occasion and perceive that the country has passed through a great revolution, and that revolution is progress. The living issues of the present time are those to which attention should be given. Having devoted much thought to them and the current of events for many previous years, I submit my views and suggestions to the public, in the hope of aiding in the dissemination of truth, and of securing in the next Congress the coöperation of those with whom I shall be associated, in well-directed efforts for the enactment of such just laws as will afford the best and most permanent relief to our country.

What is most Needed.

The first and greatest of all the changes demanding public attention is integrity in public affairs. An administration, regarding freedom of government as the right of each member to scramble for emoluments and honors for himself and party, instead of rendering faithful service to the country, has long held almost plenary possession of power. This is the most prolific source of all the national troubles. Reform in this respect is the course on which the people most strenuously insist. On this point, all, except those who are held together by the cohesive strength of plunder, are agreed. They subordinate every other question to this single one, which has now long and loudly demanded settlement. The only danger that their desired purposes may not be fulfilled, is that they may be conquered by their enemies, through the old plan of dividing those who mean well. If those who think alike will vote alike, their cause is safe. Integrity and fair dealing are so intimately blended with other sound principles in practical politics, that when this vantage-ground is gained there will be less disagreement than may be commonly expected on the other leading topics of the times, such as an honest currency, justice to the South, and a tariff alike favorable to the collection of revenue and the progress of commerce and manufactures.

Long after all pretext of temporary necessity has ceased, the country is afflicted by a debased currency of broken promises to pay, demoralization flagrantly and confessedly pervades almost every department of the national administration, in the South hostility between the races is encouraged, for the sake of the sordid profits of a few favorites of the administration it is sought to retain in power, and the mode of levying taxes was declared by the financial leader of the majority of the House of Representatives, at the last session, to be merely the result of rival grab-games for contending interests in the national legislature, which has repeatedly lent itself to fraudulent subsidies and other universally admitted perversions of public trust. Taxation and maladministration, under the present management and control, have become incomparably more oppressive than those against which our forefathers rebelled, and, unless the source of our difficulties is checked, threaten even to subvert our institutions.

Trite as it is to say that "honesty is the best policy," the essential truth has long been laid aside with many forgotten errors, and its practical application is alike the great need of the times and demand of the people. Through it only is the way to economy, diminished taxation, and renewed confidence and prosperity. In the end, it will be found to include all other public necessities. Without it there can be no reliable reform, and the people will continue to be wronged either by commending evil doctrines, or by intrigues robbing sound principles of their proper effect. Integrity in those who make our laws and manage public affairs is as needful to the well-being of the people as a firm footing and a pure atmosphere are to the progress and life of individuals.

The remedy is in the hands of the citizens. They can insist that merit—integrity and ability—not merely zeal in political intrigues, shall be the qualification for all appointments to office and retention in them. The voters need to be on their guard against the numerous class of men who estimate all things by the personal emoluments or power derived from them. Carelessness in this respect is the mainspring of all our national disgrace and disasters. No laws or institutions, however admirable, can secure the interests of the people, if they themselves become indifferent or inactive in public affairs.

The Duty of Investigation.

As the people are compelled to practice economy themselves, they expect that the administration will conform to the same standard. From

Washington and the District of Columbia to the farthest homes of the wild Indian tribes, the management of the party in power is permeated by extravagance and corruption. Exposures are sometimes made, but we have reached a period when the strongest proofs of self-convicted offense are paraded before the public gaze as proofs not of the guilt of those who are responsible for the acts, but of their virtue. Leading Republicans do not hesitate to assert that the worse their party is proved to be, the more meritorious it is. Credible assertions are made that the United States are defrauded of at least one fourth of their rightful revenue, through the misconduct of the officials intrusted with its collection. Incalculably greater injury is inflicted on the people by the preventible evils in legislation and other forms. The extent to which these have been carried can never be known unless there is a change in the *personnel* of the administration. Persevering investigation is absolutely necessary, not only to arrest the present wrongs, but as the best means of discovering the proper measures for lasting reform and improvement.

Present Embarrassments and their Causes.

The present embarrassment of our financial and commercial interests demands serious and profound attention. Its effects are felt by the people of all pursuits in every part of the Union, and, without distinction of party, they imperatively require the application of the best attainable remedy. Capital lies idle in the vaults of the banks, and is offered at lower rates of interest than at any other period in the history of this continent, while multitudes of men and women, to an extent also hitherto unparalleled, are presenting that "saddest sight on earth" of being able and anxious to work, but unable to find the work to do.

To understand the nature of the disease which is now preying on the vitals of the country, we must refer to its origin, and trace its insidious progress, reviewing the financial history of the war impartially and in the light now thrown upon it by the decisive lessons of the past.

The rebellion was precipitated on the country unexpectedly to the party in power, who were slow and unwilling to comprehend its real magnitude. The repeated prophecies of leading statesmen that it would succumb in a few weeks, are yet fresh in our memories, and will never fail to arrest the attention of all students of our history. As the nature of the impending dangers was not understood, neither the military nor pecuniary measures needed to meet them were promptly undertaken. The antiquated and exploded financial theories of obsolete European statesmen and of our own in former days, were again put into practice and once more proved to be erroneous. Those who gave more far-seeing counsels were fortunate if they escaped opprobrium. While the North believed that the crisis would rapidly pass over, the South mistakenly supposed the North would yield to its demands. The battle of Bull Run, when the Capital itself was endangered, in part dissolved the illusion on both sides; but the financial errors which had taken root were destined to be worked out to their logical results, which have now swept over the country and can only slowly be overcome. The sole consolation is that the Union has been preserved, and that by wise and honorable management, it may be restored in spirit and fact as fully as it now is materially and in form.

Financial Errors of the Republicans.

The short-sighted policy of deluding by make-shift expedients, instead of following the standard of the real and permanent good of the public, as fixed by immutable natural laws, was too conducive to the personal and partisan interests of those in power to be readily abandoned. At the extra session of Congress, in July, 1861, it was simply indicated that, in view of the expected brief duration of the war, the government would make a loan of a hundred and fifty millions in gold from the banks of New-York, Boston, and Philadelphia. Before the 17th of November, in the same year, they had actually advanced one hundred and forty-six millions in this form, and their system was so strong that after the last part of the loan had been nearly or quite paid, the gold and silver in the banks, which had at the beginning been less than fifty millions, was forty-two millions. The specie for a long time returned to the banks in the ordinary course of business. The Treasury continued to demand "thirty millions a month," and insisted that this should be paid only in coin. The banks yet had more than sufficient specie for the transaction of their own business, but further steps were taken to destroy the State banks.

The government, which should have guarded the banks carefully, so that they might have kept up the value of the currency by a knowledge of their strength, scattered the gold, and it could neither be lent over again in sufficient quantities or made available as a reserve for the banks. Suspension followed on the 31st of December, soon after the meeting of Congress, at its next regular session.

Even in the beginning of January, 1862, specie and paper money yet remained of equal value. At that date, due sagacity and prudence would have prompted the instant adoption of a system of adequate taxation and other well-considered and suitable measures of providing for the expenditures of the war. The government having, by its own action, forced the banks into suspension, authorized, on the 25th of February, 1862, a large issue of "legal tender," receivable "for all debts except duties on imports and interest on the public debt." In these notes, the distinction was, for the first time in history, made by a government between specie and its own paper. Thus the door was opened wide to the enormous over-issue of paper money, which led to the inflation of prices, and, but for our natural wealth and strongly national spirit, would have been fatal to the government and immediately disastrous to the business of the people. It was deemed more creditable to create fictitious and exaggerated prices of labor and commodities and an artificial appearance of prosperity than to enforce prompt taxation.

Billions Lost to Save One per Cent.

The administration having created an unfailing demand for gold, and fanned the fire of speculation by the terms of the original notes which were exchangeable for United States 6 per cent bonds, withdrew even this right of redemption after July 1st, 1863, and, more anxious to produce a seemingly low interest than to protect the people against an actual depreciation of the national securities, which reached the low rate of 35 cents on the dollar, made an inglorious and suicidal effort to raise loans at five per cent. The continuance of the right to exchange the "legal-tender notes" in six per cent bonds might have effectually prevented the currency from becoming redundant, as it might have been continually checked by investments in the bonds for the sake of interest. The 6 per cent bonds were sold at the rate of $1,500,000 to $2,000,000 a day—amounts nearly equal to the daily expenses of the government. Of the loan at the lower rate, little was taken except by bankers, who used the bonds in the organization of national banks. The funding was substantially arrested for several months. Many times the sum of the interest sought to be saved was lost in the enhanced rates of purchase for the army and navy, and, under a needlessly inflated currency, a war debt of over two thousand and eight hundred millions of dollars was incurred, although the value received, reckoned in gold, was probably not more than forty cents on the dollar, on all the expenditures of the war.

The currency continued to be further inflated, without any provision for converting it into interest-bearing bonds, until by the 30th June, 1864, the natural fruits of the mistaken policy became palpable to its advocates. The currency and other temporary loans amounted to over $1,125,877,034. At this crisis, Mr. Chase, in despair, resigned the Secretaryship of the Treasury.

Financial Fanaticism.

The administration having created a market for gold, with a constant supply and demand, through paying interest on bonds in gold and refusing to receive its own notes in payment of duties on imports, the congressional majority by joint resolution increased the previously extravagant duties to the amount of fifty per cent on all articles indiscriminately, for sixty-three days, ending with the 30th June, 1864. The necessary consequence was that gold rose rapidly and enormously, or rather that the currency correspondingly depreciated. Congress, alarmed and anxious to stem the tide it had thus set in motion, passed a "gold bill," approved June 17th, 1864 with the vain hope of checking the depreciation of the currency by prohibiting time contracts for the sale of gold. Violations of the act were to be punished by fines and imprisonment. The ill-advised step only added fuel to the flame. Its result was a temporary closing of the Gold-Room, leaving purchasers at the mercy of individual dealers, and, next, a mania of speculation, during which gold reached its maximum of 285, the actual premium having more than doubled within about two months. The pernicious effects of these glaring violations of the laws of common-sense and political economy were so immediately obvious that both acts were short-lived, the gold bill being repealed in fifteen days after its passage.

The protracted duration of the war, so widely at variance from the early and rose-colored assurances of the administration, added to the excessive issue of paper money, and its great depreciation induced distrust and discredit of the Union. Instead of wantonly diluting the currency and wilfully diminishing its value, so as to tempt purchasers of bonds, or, in the phraseology of the day, to "float the debt" nominally at par, but really far below it, a strong specie reserve should have been maintained, and the paper dollar kept as nearly as possible at its par value. This would have given confidence, and the people or government would have received a full and fair equivalent for the money they are compelled to pay. Throughout her recent great calamities, France, in pursuance of a policy well worthy of profound attention, never permitted her currency to reach a discount of over two and a half per cent, and yet one dollar of hard money would have bought nearly three dollars of ours, and our bonds were depreciated to a corresponding extent. No other nation has ever, during war or any other great exigency, made such distinctions, discrediting her own currency by persistently recognizing and enacting its inferiority to the precious metals.

Striking Contrast in France.

It is little to the credit of the administration, which for the last fifteen years has been intrusted with the management of our financial affairs, that, although France maintained her paper money, practically at par, during the misfortunes which ended in a loss of some of her best territory, throughout a terrific civil war, and although she paid a ransom of $1,000,000,000 and interest, our "legal tender" or government paper money is yet at a discount, varying from twelve to seventeen per cent, and gold once reached a premium of at least one hundred and eighty-five. The public debt of France is more than twice as large as our own. Her area is more than one third less than that of the State of Texas alone, and only about one twentieth part of that of the Union. Her population, long nearly stationary, and recently diminished, was, in 1872, little more than thirty-six millions, while ours is now about forty-three millions, and is probably increasing at the rate of nearly a million and a half yearly. Judging from the past, our national wealth will double in about eight years, a rate of prosperity three or four times greater than that of France. Yet, with her far inferior resources, and throughout the pressure of almost unequaled misfortunes, the outstanding issues of the Bank of France, not redeemable in specie, never exceeded $640,000,000, and were lately $489,000,000, against which it holds $307,000,000 in the precious metals, but insists, as a preliminary to the resumption of specie payments on the 1st of January, 1878, on a further reduction to the amount of nearly a hundred millions of the issues lent to the government.

Our basis of credit being, as we have seen far superior to that of France, the contrast between her financial management and that of the administration of this country deeply condemns the latter. Acting without forethought, and in one of those blunders which are sometimes said truly to be worse than crimes, it borrowed and dissipated the specie held by the banks, and paid away its own, instead of encouraging and keeping a reserve, which would have made the currency nearly at a par with coin, and thus have retained at nearly the same standard the current value of its bonds and the articles needed in the war, enormously diminishing the burdens of the people, who, through the shameless waste of their credit, now pay, in the common standard of the world, debts contracted under the fictitious valuations of an irredeemable currency, which the administration, by its example and its laws, taught the people and the world to distrust.

Our government took no efficient or well-calculated steps to keep up the value of our note circulation. But this object was the first aim of France. Our administration fed speculation, wilfully producing an artificial state of things and an appearance of prosperity which deceived many. The Secretary of the Treasury, with the hope of reducing interest, caused an immense depreciation of the currency, and brought upon us the long train of disasters from which we have not yet recovered. His was the policy of selling notes at half or one third of "their face," for the sake of saving one per cent in interest. France, on the contrary, arrested speculation by advancing the rate of interest through her bank, and kept down prices, thus encouraging exports, and enabling her government to buy at fair prices. Her financial policy was the reverse of ours, and the result was more propitious. The chief practical example she now gives as an appropriate lesson for the condition in which we are placed, is that, by means of an enlightened and moderately liberal commercial policy for the benefit of the people at large, and not the favoritism of a few, and by maintaining a large reserve of specie in her bank, she circulates free of discount a nominally inconvertible paper currency to the amount of over five hundred millions of dollars.

The Panic in 1873.

Although, owing to the unparalleled natural wealth of our country, the results of defying the positive laws of political economy were long delayed, the time necessarily came when the speculations thus set afloat were subjected to the inevitable test of realizing money from them; and it was found they rested on no adequate foundation. The administration had transferred its financial agencies to men who had been foremost in advocating its sophistries and strenuously striven to delude the people by promulgating the doctrines that "a national debt is a national blessing," and that "debt is wealth." The leading and most trusted advisers and coöperators of the government in its financial affairs became the most conspicuous speculators. The system significantly culminated in the failure of the houses which had been most highly favored and trusted by the administration. A run for deposits almost immediately followed. The sixty banks of New-York were liable for two hundred millions of dollars to their depositors. Speculation had become so rife because the currency was far in excess of legitimate commercial demands, that, to meet the emergency, the banks had depended on "call loans." The bank loans throughout the United States far exceeded those of any other date, and the ratio of cash to deposits and circulation was then, as it had been for the two previous years, less than at any other time during the last forty years. In New-York, within little more than three weeks, the "legal tender" reserve was reduced from thirty-four millions to less than six millions. The securities on which the "call loans" had been made became unsalable, except at ruinous prices.

Collapse of Unprofitable Speculations.

Prominent among the results of the stimulation of a false currency was a mania for the construction of railroads, which averaged nearly six thousand miles for the five years ended in the crisis, against an average of about eleven hundred in the seven years ended with 1866. The reaction was so disastrous that railroad bonds to the amount of $567,028,639 were in default, and considerably less than half of the railroad stocks in the whole country paid dividends, entailing losses and ruin on multitudes of innocent sufferers. These disasters, though more easily computed than many others and larger in amount than any other single class, are probably little more than fair specimens of the wide-spread calamities. Many manufactures, notably those of iron, cotton, and wool, were suspended or put on short time. Laboring men and women were thrown out of work to an extent previously unknown in the history of our country; immigration, that prolific source of our prosperity, decreased; multitudes returned to Europe to spread abroad in every land the tidings of their disappointments and deter others from embarking; and the number of bankruptcies in 1873, as also in 1874, exceeded that ever before known, except in 1861, the year when the memorable destruction of trade and capital was caused by the war. From that time to this, the commercial confidence necessary to the employment of labor has been impaired, and the poverty of the masses and crime have increased beyond all former precedent. All the calamities we now endure would have been incalculably more general and severe but for the prompt action of the Clearing-House. through which, when the crisis occurred, the stronger banks of New-York combined to sustain the weaker by combining their reserves of legal-tender notes and issuing interest-bearing loan certificates, which were made the media for the payment of differences.

The Law of Financial Panics.

It is instructive to note that throughout the history of our country, commercial panics have universally followed large expansions of the currency. By unsettling values and stimulating wild and reckless speculations, which, but for a superfluity of the circulating medium, would never be undertaken, they draw money away from sound investments which would yield permanent profit to those who make them with a view to enriching themselves by rendering real services to the people at large. The national industry has been misdirected—a course analogous to waste of time and money misspent by an individual. The violent and well-remembered panic of 1837 followed an increase of $54,796,320—or from $94,389,570 to $149,185,000—in the circulation within the brief period of three years, while during the same period the loans and discounts, which practically are for many purposes a part of the currency, increased $200,996,261, or from $326,119,441 on the 1st of January, 1834, to $525,115,702 on the corresponding day in 1837. Until seventeen years afterward, the aggregate of the loans and discounts of the banks never were so great as in 1837. In 1857, the year of the next great panic, they had increased to $684,456,887, and in the two preceding years the currency had increased from $186,952,223 to $214,778,822. In 1860, the paper currency was $207,100,000, but in 1866, under the Republican *régime*, the outstanding circulation had increased to $648,866,000, and on July 1, 1875, to $727,640,588, exclusive of over forty-one millions of fractional currency.

The Experience of Mankind.

It may be freely admitted that, at first sight, the theory that paper promises to pay are capital, is not without some show of plausibility. Currency is the symbol of wealth, and the shadow is frequently mistaken for the substance. It is, in fact, when inflated, nothing more than so much "watered stock." The value is nominally increased, but the actual property remains the same. Sooner or later, the fraud is exposed, but from time to time this is again forgotten, and a new era of inflation and delusion begins to end in the same way as its predecessors. The experiment has often been made, and as often attended by the same bitter lessons. Yet, with new men, the old errors are repeated. Happily for mankind, nations are long-lived, seldom dying, and in some degree the wisdom gained by one generation filters down the course of time to its successors. As, on some points, the laws of finance are as positive as those of physical nature, the experience of other countries is instructive.

Financial Principles in England.

In 1797, the Bank of England began, under authority of Parliament, to issue excessive amounts of notes which the London merchants agreed to receive at par. Even this could not prevent their depreciation. Parliament seconded the ineffectual efforts, and, in 1811, passed the celebrated resolution that "the price of gold had advanced, but the value of bank-notes was not depreciated"—a complete counterpart to the declaration of one of our own secretaries of the Treasury, who claimed to be the author of the legal-tender system, that gold had increased in value, but that his paper money had not depreciated. In 1814, a British "gold bill" was passed, enacting that "the taking of gold coin at more than its value, or bank-notes at less, shall be deemed a misdemeanor." It was as ineffectual as our own. The trade in the precious metals was conducted as openly as ever, and the depreciation of the notes continued. No effort was made to enforce the impotent law.

The notes remained below par for nineteen years. At last the celebrated "Bullion Committee," appointed by Parliament to investigate the calamitous condition of British financial affairs and their inconsistency with the theories too generally believed, recognized the actual depreciation, and declared that this was the cause of the general advance in prices. Its main conclusion was that "the country ought to be brought back with as much speed as is compatible with a wise caution, to the original principle of cash payments, at the option of the holders of bank-notes." The following axioms were regarded as incontrovertibly established:

If gold is at a premium in paper, the paper is redundant and depreciated, the premium measures the depreciation.

If the inferior currency be removed, the exchanges will be turned, the overflow will stop, and, if any vacuum is created, gold will flow in to supply it.

A better and a worse currency can not circulate together. The worse will drive out the better.

The Governor and Deputy-Governor of the Bank of England, the Chancellor of the Exchequer, the other highest officials of the day, the London bankers, and the people in general, opposed the sound views of the committee, and Parliament itself repudiated them. The nation at large, with the exception of a few thinking men, long continued to reassert that the large volume of the currency had nothing to do with the rise in prices; that the bank-notes had lost nothing of their value, and that no restriction of the circulation was needed.

In eight years afterward, the public had been instructed by the logic of events, and, with few exceptions—which, however, included the Directors of the Bank of England—the truth of the doctrines held by the committee was universally admitted. Robert Peel himself, although he had held the opinions of the previous Parliamentary majority, and voted with it, became one of the most distinguished advocates of the committee, with a mind ever open to conviction and a firmness and integrity of purpose which gave him strength never to flinch from retracting erroneous views. In opening the debate of 1819, he said:

He was ready to avow, without shame or remorse, that he went into the committee with a very different opinion from that which he at present entertained, for his views on the subject were most materially different when he voted against the resolutions brought forward in 1811 by Mr. Horner, as the Chairman of the Bullion Committee. Having gone into the inquiry determined to dismiss all former impressions which he might have received. . . . . he had resolved . . . . to adopt every inference which authentic information or mature reflection should offer to his mind.

The views of the committee have long continued to be, in substance, the laws of finance in Great Britain; and for more than thirty years the use of bank-checks and other modern means of facilitating payments has been so great that there has been no material increase in her paper currency, although during the same time her commercial transactions have been multiplied fourfold.

The Warnings of France.

The depreciation of the currency of France under the regency of Louis the Fifteenth has become proverbial. At its origin it had its advocates, but although France prohibited the use of coin and decreed even the penalty of death for those who refused to receive the paper at par, it fell until the equivalent of a hundred dollars in our money would buy only a single pound of butter. At last it became utterly worthless ; the people by common consent returned to a specie currency ; and the author of the scheme only escaped from the country at the peril of his life.

Bitter Experience of Austria.

Austria has been slower to learn, and her disasters have been prolonged to a much more recent date. Sixty-five years ago, her currency was so far reduced in value that she issued " redemption notes," in which it was to be " redeemed " at the rate of three to one. This having failed, she over and over again, under new names, such as " Viennese legal tender " and " anticipation notes," vainly sought to provide substitutes for a metallic standard. In 1873 she suffered from a panic bearing a close resemblance to our own. After her war of 1866, large issues of paper money were made, which led to a belief in the abundance of capital and to speculations of all kinds. The government itself gave aid by guaranteeing dividends on various railroads. The market was glutted with an immense quantity of so-called securities, in which it was for the time impracticable to distinguish between the good and the bad. The inevitable crash ensued. As in this country, the leading speculators were the first to suspend. Their example was soon followed by a multitude of smaller operators. Even the strong houses were shaken. The Bourse was closed to prevent violence among its more adventurous members, some of whom committed suicide.

Events in Early American History.

In the yet brief history of the United States and Canada, the same lesson has been no less imperatively taught. I pass over the examples to be found in the records of the individual States and colonies. Franklin himself, early in the Revolutionary War, warmly approved the issue of bills " on the faith of the continent." One member of the Congress, who seems to have been alone in his views or in the courage needed to avow them, urged taxation, but was bluffed by one of the almost unanimous majority, who, in a spirit of which we have conspicuous examples in our own time, asked, " if he was to help to tax the people, when they could go to the printer's office and get a cart-load of money." The currency decreased in value until monstrous sums were needed to buy a cow or procure a frugal meal. It became exchangeable only at the rate of a thousand dollars for one sound dollar. This too in spite of penal laws to enforce the impracticable wishes of Congress. The historian of the time says :

"Wealth was accumulated by the dishonest multitudes of contractors, and the many defrauders of that unhappy period, while more deserving men felt that it had been plundered from their own coffers for the aggrandizement of such people."

No thoughtful statesman ever overlooks the precedents establishing the positive conclusion that wherever legislators have attempted by penalties to compel the people to take irredeemable paper at par with coin, the laws of the strongest alike with the weakest governments have signally failed in enforcing their wishes.

Responsibility of the Republicans.

There is no more striking instance of the forgetfulness of yet recent history and the superficial consideration, too often with the most deplorable results, given to the affairs which concern us all, than the impression on the minds of some candid men, and the loud and reiterated assertions of others, that the Democrats are the party of inflation, and the Republicans are the most reliable supporters of a sound currency and a return to specie payment. The traditional policy of the Democrats is that of a currency redeemable in hard money, and will be so to the end. Individuals are to be found who on other points agree with them, but believe in the pernicious doctrine of an irredeemable currency. They are not the party, and misrepresent its well-known and hitherto universally admitted tenets. On the other hand, the Republicans, from the beginning of their possession of power to the present time, have uniformly practiced the fraud, and attempted to justify it, until their efforts were no longer availing. They took from the banks the power of paying in specie, are responsible for the whole existing system of paper money, and their leaders have wrangled among themselves for the honor of its authorship.

Some, although holding general allegiance to the Republican party, were so far patriotic and wise as to warn it against the cause from which most of our financial evils sprang, and have since wrung from it spasmodic promises of reform which have been as often broken, thus proving the utter want of reliability in the Republican organization.

There are many conspicuous instances of this practical deception. One of them was the first act of Congress approved by President Grant after his inauguration. In clear and terse words, it explicitly "declared that the faith of the United States is solemnly pledged to the payment in coin or its equivalent of the United States notes," and that Congress "pledges its faith to make provision at the earliest practicable period for the redemption of the United States notes in coin." The hopes thus given were fallacious. The congressional majority arrested the contraction begun by McCulloch when secretary of the Treasury, and supported the illegal inflation by Boutwell and his successor. Five years ago, in 1870, the premium on gold fell to eight and a half per cent, and yet it was recently seventeen and a half. During this period, under Republican control, paper money has receded further from approaching to an equalization with gold.

In the last session of Congress, the Republican party again repeated its delusive pledges, by announcing that in four years specie payments should be renewed, but accompanying the resolution by no adequate measures for fulfilling the promise previously so often broken, and their chief financial leader in the Senate repeatedly refused to state what would be the operations of the bill he introduced. Such acts are plainly nothing more than attempts to deceive the people, and by seeming compliance circumvent their efforts for the return to an honest and substantial currency.

Whatever show of reason existed during the war in favor of an inflated paper currency now no longer exists, but the supporters of a sound and fixed standard of value have again and again been outwitted, betrayed, and outvoted by those who falsely professed to be the friends of redemption, and in co-operation with weak, though more sincere men, who, fearful of injuring their party, and preferring its life to the claims of their country, let "I dare not wait upon I would," have made the promise to the ear, but always broken it to the sense. The party is the same now as ever, whatever may be the views and wishes of some of its members.

Necessity of a Fixed Standard.

Stripped of the sophistries with which it is frequently surrounded, the necessity of a fixed standard of value in all the commercial and monetary affairs of the nation is so clear that he who runs may read it. Paper money may be freely used; checks or bills of exchange, aided by the railroad, telegraph, and post-office, may transact nearly all such business of the country as is on a large scale, and tend to prevent any exorbitant rate of interest; but it is essential that all these means should simply represent one universal and uniform standard. Without this guard, they become uncontrollable and unsound—extortionate taskmasters instead of good and faithful servants.

In the minds of many men affairs of state are surrounded with a confusing mystery, as if the principles of ordinary facts and common-sense could not be applied to them. Yet it is plain that trade in grain of any kind would be placed under such enormous disadvantages as to render it almost impossible if the bushel measure of to-day might be larger or smaller to-morrow from causes the farmer or merchant could not foresee and altogether independent of their control. The dealers in textile fabrics, and in land itself, would be in strange predicaments if the yard and the foot were subject to great and frequent variations, and might represent at one time little more than a third of their measure at another. Yet the obstacle which has been thrown in the way of the trade and prosperity of the country is almost exactly of the same nature. The "legal tender" dollar at one time was worth little more than a third of the true dollar, and continually changes from day to day, making trade uncertain and values of all kinds doubtful. No man knows when he rises what they may be that morning, or when he goes to his place of business what they may be before the sun sets. It is an established fact that the greatest possible certainty of value is attainable only by enforcing the standard of the precious metals; they become the property of whatever nation or individual will give most for them. Their portability and the universal recognition of their value throughout the world make them the natural and least fluctuating medium of exchange, and arbitrary legislation has been and seemingly always will be unsuccessful in discovering or enforcing any stable substitute for them.

The people are vitally interested in a return to a specie basis. The paper they now receive for services, daily toil, and general business purposes, is worth only eighty-five cents on the dollar, through its depreciation to that extent below gold value, which they pay for nearly all the articles required for daily use. No sophistry can long continue to delude them, while a vigilant press penetrates the remotest parts of the country, into a belief that such depreciated and inconvertible paper money is the best currency.

The notion of many of the advocates of expansion is vaguely that it would be substantially a distribution of money among the masses at large; but it is, in fact, one of the most seductive methods of depriving those who depend on their labor and industry of their just reward, placing colossal fortunes in the hands of a few, to whom it gives a lion's share of the little the people individually possess, taxing their labor and that of their descendants, and thus endangering even the republic and the liberties of the people. This has been the uniform experience of mankind, and it is aptly illustrated by the history of our country in the last fifteen years, during which we have had an irredeemable circulation, and when, while wealth slipped more rapidly than ever into the hands of speculators, the number of bankruptcies exceeded those of any former term, and poverty, distress, and crime have made alarming progress unprecedented in the history of our country.

The Present Time is Opportune.

The present time is the most opportune we have had, since inflation began, for making vigorous preparations for specie payments. The premium on gold has been reduced by commercial causes, apart from legislation, from 185½ to 12 or 17 per cent, thus indicating that the remaining steps to gold at a par rate with notes can gradually be safely retraced, by no extraordinary amount of statesmanship, provided it is sincere and persevering. Since the war began, the circulating medium has increased three times as fast as the population. In New-York, the accumulation of money and the low rate at which it may be had are unprecedented; but few borrowers whom the capitalists will trust are to be found. Low as the rate of interest throughout the world has long been, money was for several months cheaper in New-York than in the great cosmopolitan market of London, the difficulty of our capitalists having been to find profitable employment for their currency at home. A similar state of affairs prevails, though in a minor degree, at Chicago, Cincinnati, and the other great financial centres of the Union. Even the bill passed June 20th, 1874, with the intention of increasing the currency, has proved, as clearly as the thermometer shows temperature, that more is not needed, and that there is a redundancy above the wants of the people. Under its operations, and after allowing for the new circulation, there has been a net contraction of the paper currency to the amount of over fifteen millions, within a year. Banks are unable to employ their money at fair profits. The legal tender and other reserves held by the banks of New-York at the time of my writing exceed $82,000,000. The abundance of money throughout the civilized world affords peculiarly favorable opportunities for funding or obtaining specie and foreign credits, which, to a certain extent, are identical with each other. The futility of expanding the currency was signally demonstrated when the Secretary of the Treasury, during the panic of 1873, issued, without authority of law, $26,000,000 of notes, in the vain hope of relieving the money market. These notes did not enter at all into the general circulation, but were hoarded by savings-banks and trust companies, as were those which had been already withdrawn from the banks of discount and deposit. Large exportations of grain to Europe from this side of the Atlantic are expected. Our imports have enormously shrunk. The people themselves are more than usually free from debt; and last, but not least, is the encouraging fact that their minds have been long and carefully prepared by an increasingly intelligent press, never before so sound and well-informed on financial topics, to take more than superficial views and look beyond the delusions of what is merely immediate and temporary to that which, though slightly more remote, is permanent and real. The government, at present unable to redeem its promises to pay, may never again have so good an opportunity of beginning the process of exchanging its bonds at a low rate of interest, or the national banks of laying up the reserves of specie, on which, in their hands, under the wholesome law of free competition, the restoration of prosperity depends.

On the other hand, if the policy of the expansionists could be followed, the return to specie payments and the successful funding of the debt, long ago due on demand, but yet unpaid, will become more and more difficult, until, as we have seen has repeatedly been the case in other countries and our own, the control of legislation will be lost, broken promises will be renewed only by making more of them, and wide-spread disaster, misery, repudiation, and national dishonor will ensue. We have reached a point where any expansion of an irredeemable currency means its indefinite increase, and are approaching that crisis against which the united wisdom of many generations warns us, in the maxim that the descent to destruction is easy, but the labor and work of retracing our steps is difficult if not impossible.

We have now arrived at the period when inflation no longer inflates. In the body political and financial, as in the human body, there is a point where the power of stimulants ceases and can no longer prevent collapse. This is the law of all serious panics and their results. There is a great shrinkage in business, and no important revival can be expected until a new financial system which will deserve and receive public confidence is fairly begun. In proportion as there is a cry for inflation, capital, proverbially timid, seeks for safety, withdraws from enterprise, and refuses to employ labor. Until the future policy of the government is permanently settled, there will be no real renewal of the commercial and general prosperity of the country.

The Increase of Currency.

Some are under an impression that the currency has already been very largely contracted. In support of this theory, reference is made to the temporary loans, certificates of indebtedness, etc., existing in 1865, and afterward funded. These were, in no proper sense, the currency of the country. If they were, they would simply prove that contraction on a vast scale can be rapidly made without injury to the people, the panic not having taken place until eight years afterward, and the Secretary of the Treasury, in his report of November 30th, 1867, having been justified in saying, "While this has been accomplished, there has been no commercial crisis, and (outside of the Southern States, which are still greatly suffering from the effects of the war and the unsettled state of their industrial interests and political affairs) no considerable financial embarrassment." The same testimony was repeated in the report of the following year. It will be seen, by the figures already presented, that, instead of contraction, an increase of seventy-eight millions of circulation occurred between April 1st, 1866, and July 1st, 1875.

When Can we Resume?

The Act of January 14th, 1875, passed by the last Republican Congress, under the previous question, cutting off all debate, has done more than any other single measure to produce expansionists. It has created alarm in business circles, and given to inflation an importance it could not otherwise have attained. The impression is that if the act is rigidly enforced, the contraction of the currency will of necessity be so rapid as to produce again widespread disaster, and such undoubtedly would be the case if *resumption were really enforced at the date named for it, January* 1, 1879. Fortunately for the people, a new Congress intervenes, and a modification of this law will no doubt be effected, more in consonance with the true interests of the country. The time when paper will be at par with gold is so far remote that not a few of the leading statesmen who most desire it despair of living to see their hopes fulfilled. I express only the general sentiment of the most sagacious financiers in saying that the consummation can not be reached for many years.

How to Resume.

The expediency of a return to specie payments may now be taken for granted. The next step for the people and Congress is the consideration of the best means for accomplishing it with the least possible disturbance of existing interests. On this point, there must naturally be a difference of opinion, but there will ultimately be no lack of unanimity after due discussion in a candid and deliberative spirit. I have shown that there has been during the past year, notwithstanding the power to expand under existing laws, a voluntary withdrawal of the circulation to the extent of about $15,000,000 ; it is believed that this process will continue by reason of the excess now held by the banks for which there is no employment. If, in addition to this, the government should authorize the purchase and cancellation of some moderate amount, say $1,000,000 per month, of the legal-tender notes, and authorize the Secretary of the Treasury to sell five per cent bonds of the United States, to provide funds for that object, the first great step would be taken toward resumption, without injury to the financial and business interests of the country. Under the recommendations of Mr. McCulloch, when Secretary of the Treasury, contraction on a larger scale was begun, but Congress, fearful of the effect, withdrew its assent. I propose that the rate and method of contraction shall be so gradual that Congress can have no excuse for again intervening. Rigid adherence to such a course would indicate a determination to return to a sound basis; *the absence of the inferior currency would be gradually supplied by the superior;* the problem as to the method of resumption would be solved, and the system work itself out by a natural process, while individuals and the banks would have ample time to prepare for a new condition of affairs. Business being thus adjusted upon the new basis, confidence would return, and with it prosperity would soon prevail. The act of January 14th, 1875, should be modified in conformity with this view.

More "Legal Tender" Illegal.

Gold by the Constitution of the United States is a legal tender, and, as a necessary consequence, the standard of value. That instrument gives no authority or power to any department of the government to issue legal tender paper, or a currency payable on demand. The only ground upon which it was issued during the civil war was that of seeming necessity, it being supposed that the existence and supremacy of the government were involved. Without entering into the conflicting decisions of the Supreme Court of the United States, it is sufficient to know that they indorsed the issue of legal tender, but only as a war necessity. It necessarily follows it could not otherwise be legally issued. We now find many demanding a withdrawal of the bank-note circulation, and a further issue of legal tender. Under a proper construction of the Constitution, this is impossible, and, as Democrats adhere to that instrument, they can not for a moment contend for such a proposition, and if they did, their efforts would be unavailing.

When the legal tender issued by the government is withdrawn, it must cease to issue more or any paper currency whatever.

Beware of Arbitrary Power.

The right to control the financial affairs of the country by increasing the circulating medium at his own will, is too dangerous a power to be lodged in the hands of the Secretary of the Treasury. That high official is seldom chosen for his adaptation to the special duties devolved upon him. He may be one who has attained political rank through his merit as a lawyer and speaker, while, according to his own frank assertions, he is profoundly ignorant of the simplest facts and principles in modern finance, and may be induced to take a course exactly the reverse of his own most cherished convictions. Sometimes the Secretary of the Treasury may be a mere partisan intriguer or profoundly ignorant tool. At another time, the holder of that office may be a man of sterling principles, sound doctrines, and pure character; but, in the changes of parties, there can be no certainty of this; while, although the evil may never again reach the criminal magnitude to which it has attained under a Republican administration, we may be sure that so long as unwarrantable power is placed in his hands, he will continually be interviewed by astute speculators, and that all possible means of wealth and perverted intellect will be employed in artifices to persuade him to use his power for the promotion of special and individual interests, rather than for the public good. Hence, the aim of all good citizens should be to separate the government from the business of banking. It can not remain in the hands of the government without creating such centralization and influences as are hostile to the spirit and perpetuation of republican institutions.

Upon the withdrawal or redemption of the legal tender, and the resumpion of specie payment, the issue of new currency should be practically free to the banks to any extent on the deposit of national bonds as security for the circulation. Under these conditions, there would be free trade in money. The law of supply and demand would solve the question of the currency, and the largest practicable amount of benefit the banks can render would be attained, while the circulation would be kept within moderate limits, and gradually attain the true and honest standard of the world. As one of the ultimate results, the time may come when their notes, amply secured by government bonds, in a proportion which will assuredly command specie, may be accepted by the government in payment of its dues, and re-issued for its current expenses.

Payment of the National Debt.

Notwithstanding the small amount received for the national debt, the honor and credit of the nation require that its interest and principal shall be paid in coin. The life of the nation was preserved, and an impetus which has generally been recognized was given to the great cause of self-government. But the further extinction of the debt should be suspended until a return to specie payment. The people, without regard to party, united with great promptitude and bravery in the preservation of the Union, and submitted to the most exorbitant taxation and exactions without a murmur. When the war was over, it was generally expected that heavy taxation would cease; but, instead of this, the burdens have continued, and seven hundred millions of direct and indirect taxes, besides the needlessly exorbitant and profligate cost of collecting them, have been taken from the people to diminish a debt, payment of which could well have been postponed until the financial condition of the country would better have enabled our citizens to meet it. The determination of the people to pay the debt, the known magnitude of our resources, and the rapidity of their development, are such, that after the resumption of specie payment, its gradual reduction may be anticipated.

Need of a Revenue Tariff.

The discussions which have engaged so large a share of public attention, as to the opposing doctrines of free trade and "protection," are now of diminished importance. The taxation needed for the expenses of government and interest on the national debt is already so burdensome that argument as to the expediency of levying further taxes on the many, for the benefit of the few, should by common consent be postponed. Revenue with the least possible injury to the people is the proper object of the tariff. This was avowed in the first revision by the Republicans, in 1861, but under this disguise, the Congressional majority, through the influence of special interests, made the income of the government a secondary affair, needlessly increased prices, and made almost impossible an exchange of various articles we were accustomed to export, besides impeding the exportation of many others.

In numerous instances, the duties are so heavy that revenue from them is almost entirely destroyed. The duty, on many articles absolutely necessary, is practically prohibitory while the people are compelled to pay enhanced prices to the manufacturers. Thus, on blankets, the duty collected in 1873 was $6,337, not far from the whole amount of the importations, which was only $7,940. The total consumption of blankets is credibly estimated to have been $20,000,000, of which, through the prices created by the tariff, the consumers paid to the manufacturers $18,000,000 more than they would have paid in the open markets of the world. The prices of tools and simple materials used by mechanics are increased in the same way. The duty collected on saws was $7,630,on importations to the value of $19,033, forcing the payment of $1,200,000, under pretense of revenue and protection. Under the same system of favoritism and prohibition, our builders and others who use wood-screws were needlessly forced to pay $1,400,000 for the benefit of a few persons especially interested in their manufacture. The burden, of course, falls ultimately on the citizens at large. Abuses of this kind have gone on so long unchecked and encouraged that the financial leader of the majority in the House of Representatives does not hesitate to denounce the whole system of taxation as controlled by the intrigues of rings and cliques, without regard to principles or the interests of the people. Obviously the tariff needs thorough revision and reform.

Encouragement to Home Industry.

So long as our observation of the prices we are compelled to pay on the articles we use or consume is confined to our own country only we lose sight of their injurious effect. When we compare prices in our own country with those of the world at large, we ascertain our condition with tolerable precision. The competition to which our shipping is subjected on the ocean, in trade with other countries, affords a strong illustration of this rule. Before

1860, 75 to 80 per cent of our foreign commerce was in American vessels. The proportions are now almost literally reversed; over 72 per cent being carried in the vessels of other countries. Of our whole foreign carrying trade, little more than one fourth is under our own flag. The earnings of the trade were recently estimated by the Secretary of the Treasury to be more than a hundred millions of dollars yearly. In 1872, the amount paid to foreign steamships for freight and passage money, was $134,742,441. When we consider that such sums are paid annually, and that our ship-owners, sailors, and others formerly enjoyed the pre-eminence and chief profits in a trade now so nearly monopolized by foreigners, and of which our citizens are deprived by what are termed "protective laws," it is plain that a liberal and comprehensive change is needed in legislation. Upon similar principles, judiciously applied, a strong stimulus could be given to the exports of many manufactures, and the additional labor employed in their production would increase the demand for agricultural products, and the home consumption of those manufactures to which the condition of our country is specially adapted. The exorbitant rates of many duties are not only unfair to the public at large, and especially so to the farmer, the prices of whose productions are mainly regulated by those in other countries, but create temptations which have been amply proved to demoralize the public servants, and by encouraging smuggling and fraudulent valuations to an unprecedented extent—asserted by a leading Republican to be 67 per cent—wring high prices from the pockets of the people, for the benefit of criminals, while the government receives comparatively small returns.

Principles of the British Tariff.

The theory of protecting and encouraging industry by high duties, levied, in the main, from the industrious, has long been tried, while no legislative efforts have been made to attain the same object by the judicious application of the lowest taxation consistent with the needful revenue. In this respect, the cause to which Great Britain is indebted for her manufacturing and commercial prosperity is well worthy of study. While our tariff levies duties on nearly two thousand five hundred different and distinctly enumerated articles or classes of articles, the whole British tariff includes only fourteen; all others are supplied to her consumers free of duty. Although we can not yet attain the same simplicity, it would be wise to take steps in that direction. A better and more moderate tariff, while yielding an ample revenue, would give our home producers many advantages. It is calculated that by such a change, aided by a sound currency, our manufacturers would be enabled to supply the agricultural, commercial, manufacturing, and other consumers of their goods, at rates varying from 25 to 50 per cent lower than at present. They would share in the general relief of the people, and their business would rest on a solid basis. It is worth while to try the experiment of giving every man who has a dollar to spend, the largest possible returns for it.

An American Continental System.

Concurrently with a tariff reform, which would encourage our manufacturers and commerce and relieve our agricultural interests, steps should be taken, in view of extending to Canada, Cuba, and Mexico, the freedom of trade which already exists throughout the United States from the Atlantic to the Pacific, and from Canada to our Southern boundaries, and is universally admitted to be indispensable to the prosperity of our people. There is no reason why a free exchange of the products of labor between our own people and those of neighboring countries would not be at least as advantageous to all the parties concerned, as that between the citizens of our various States is to them. On our Northern and Southern frontier, the full commercial and manufacturing development of our territory has been greatly retarded and injured by the mutual but unnatural prohibition of free trade with neighbors who live close to our own doors, although under other governments.

Many of our statesmen, instead of attempting to confer these great boons on their country, fixed their eyes on a frivolous extension of trade with small remote countries, with which our dealings must always be insignificant. A commercial treaty was lately made, by a triumphant vote, with the Sandwich Islands, while the opportunities of establishing similar relations with larger and nearer countries were entirely neglected. Yet last year, our whole trade with those islands amounted to much less than two millions of dollars, while, even under the present oppressive restrictions, our trade with the North-American British possessions, Cuba, and Mexico, was over a hundred times as large, having exceeded two hundred and eight millions, and might, by a removal of commercial barriers, be extended to double that amount.

Extension of Trade with Canada.

During the last session of Congress, proposals for the extension of our trade with Canada received considerable attention from the press and many commercial bodies in this country and the Dominion, and were brought before the Senate. Objections were made against the proposed treaty, but no serious effort was made to carry out a principle undoubtedly advantageous to both countries, whatever the merits of the particular measure may have been. The magnitude of the question is little understood. The British North-American possessions contain an area of three million, four hundred and seventy-eight thousand, three hundred and eighty square miles, more than is owned by the United States, exclusive of Alaska, and not much less than the whole of Europe, with its family of nations. Their population is now not far from five millions.

The best solution of the subject would undoubtedly be the adoption of an American system of commercial union similar to that of the German Zollverein, under which duties are collected only on the outside frontier of the States which are parties to it, the revenue is equitably divided, and trade between them is as free and untrammeled as among the several States of our own Union. There would be an enormous and immediate saving in the abolition of the frontier custom-houses between the people of both countries, the extension of trade would have a most favorable influence on the prosperity of all the parties to the arrangement, and, through the renewed impulses and life thus given trade with other countries would be extended, with wide-spread benefits to the world at large.

So long ago as 1864, a majority vote of the House of Representatives testified that it was decidedly in favor of amending and extending the provisions of the former reciprocity treaty, in consonance with concurrent resolutions adopted by the Legislature of the State of New-York, and expressing a strong desire for the removal of all artificial barriers to trade between the United States and Canada; but the war intervened, and no further progress was then made. From that time to the present, notwithstanding the numerous appeals to Congress by various commercial and other bodies of the highest character, the subject has been neglected and not even fully discussed.

The best practical course appears to be the appointment of efficient commissioners by both countries to ascertain whether a customs' union can be established, and, if this is impracticable, to ascertain by careful scrutiny, item by item, in what articles reciprocally free trade between the two countries would be mutually advantageous. Our people would doubtless profit by being enabled to buy lumber of all kinds free of duty. Our supplies of it are rapidly diminishing; it is needed on every farm and in every house, and is the basis of many articles for export and home consumption. On the other hand, the exportation of many of our manufactures to Canada might be greatly increased if admitted into that country free of duty.

Unsatisfactory Relations with Cuba.

Our commerce with Cuba has long been in a very unsatisfactory condition. Our importations from her last year amounted to the large sum of $86,272,466, while our exports of domestic origin to her were only $19,597,-981; the balance of $66,674,485—except less than two millions of foreign goods exported from this country—was necessarily paid in gold or its equivalent in bills of exchange on other countries. No point in our foreign relations is more worthy of attention than this. The vast sum thus paid yearly to Cuba would soon enable us to resume specie payments if we could pay it in the products of our industry in other forms. It is believed that much might be done in this direction by an honorable treaty with Spain, tending not only to the commercial benefit of all parties concerned, but to terminate the unfortunate relations between her and Cuba by harmonizing their mutual interests.

Our Trade with Mexico.

The people and government of Mexico, like those of Canada, are undoubtedly desirous of wider commercial intercourse. Our trade with them is certain to attain gigantic proportions at no distant day. The same general principles which should regulate our policy with Canada should also guide us in our relations with Mexico. We should not covet their territory but desire their trade and the harmonious development of our various resources, leaving us free from the responsibility and burden of managing their affairs, and, least of all, should we, by money wrung from the pockets of our already overtaxed citizens, endeavor to annex foreign territory, or any part of it, and give others a share in governing us. The certainty of an economical, free, and pure government should be the attraction on which we rely. Admission into the Union should be regarded as a privilege, not as a matter of bargain and sale.

The trade we might soon have with Mexico is of incalculable importance. She is capable of supplying our rapidly increasing population with tropical productions for centuries to come. Last year, our imports of the products of the sugar-cane from Cuba alone amounted to $75,728,448, while those from all other countries were only $17,120,755. Yet the supply of these necessary articles from Cuba is liable to be cut off almost at any time by the emancipation of the slaves, through whose labor it is produced. The same immediate results which followed emancipation in the other West-Indian islands must be expected in Cuba. It is, therefore, advisable that, with wise foresight, we should provide other sources of supply. Mexico alone can furnish them, and she can do so abundantly. Her population already amounts to 9,000,000, being six times as large as that of Cuba, which is 1,500,000—a fair index to the probable consumption of our products by the people of the two countries under similar conditions of trade. Hitherto her industrial development has been materially crippled by the absence of cheap transportation for her products from the rich lands of the interior. Railroads are now removing this obstacle, and their construction affords the best opportunity that will ever arise for us to open a mutually beneficial exchange of the products of the industry of our people for many articles now of prime necessity, and which we can not advantageously raise in our own country but are abundantly produced in Mexico.

Under a good commercial treaty or customs' union with Mexico, many years would not elapse before her territory would be intersected with a network of railways carrying prosperity into every part, the amount of our productions taken in exchange for hers would far exceed the enormous sum now paid annually to Cuba, and the difficulties arising from the Libra Zona or Free Belt on our frontier would immediately be settled; while the more remote political results which would arise from the increased intercourse of the people of both countries, through the development of their natural commercial union, must be obvious to all thinking men.

It should also be remembered that by the adoption of an American commercial system, we should not only supersede the demand upon us for the specie or bills of exchange now paid for tropical productions, but become also the intermediate carriers and factors for the trade which would be indefinitely extended between our neighbors in Canada on the north and those in Mexico on the south. The Canadians, by their recent proposals for a treaty of trade with the United States, and the Mexicans, by the liberal concessions their government has made, providing for a railroad nearly seven hundred miles in length, from the city of Leon to connect with the International Railroad of Texas, and thus with the railway system of the United States, prove their appreciation of the benefits to be derived from enlarged commercial intercourse with our citizens, who, we may be sure, will not transact business if it is not to their profit.

Best Policy toward the South.

The rule that "honesty is the best policy" is, perhaps, even more obviously true in its application to the treatment of the South than to affairs of the tariff and finance. The manufacture of false reports of Southern outrages has run its course, been detected and exposed, and is no longer profitable to the seekers of Northern favor. The misgovernment of our Southern fellow-citizens has become so palpable that not a few of the Republicans themselves see it is not so much the Southern people as the party in power that needs reformation. One of their chief leaders acknowledges that "it is not the disease but the doctors that we ought to examine—it is not the illness but the medicine that does the harm." The administration has steadfastly followed the course of those disreputable practitioners who administer drugs to drive a patient into madness, and keep him in confinement under false certificates, knowing that their occupation and fees will be at an end when his actual condition is known.

Considered only as a matter of self-interest, the prosperity of the South is of incalculable importance to the Northern people. One of the great causes of stagnation in the Northern manufactories is the impoverished condition of the South. According to the census of the United States, the production of the great staple of cotton, so important for home use and in our foreign exchanges, shrank from nearly five millions and a half of bales in 1860, to little over three millions in 1870. The production of tobacco decreased in far larger proportions. These losses are not counterbalanced by any increase in other articles. The production of the cereals decreased forty-four per cent, and the value of live stock twenty-six per cent. All this is in strong contrast to the prosperity of the previous decade.

Carpet-Bag Spoliation.

Part of the evil influence of the infamous adventurers who have been aided by the civil power of the administration and the army itself, and have united with the managers of their party elsewhere to use the colored vote, first to control and rob the South, next to aid in governing and despoiling the people of the North, is clearly shown by an examination of the debts and liabilities incurred in the Southern States since the close of the war. At that time, the amount in Georgia and Texas was merely nominal, but on January 1st, 1872, as shown in the Ku-Klux Report of that year, it was over fifty millions in the former and twenty millions in the latter State. Since the war ended, up to January, 1870, the debts and liabilities of the various

Southern States grew from eighty-seven millions to three hundred and sixty-two millions—a net increase of over two hundred and seventy-five millions. This vast sum has mainly been squandered or stolen, not fairly invested for the benefit of the people to whom it belonged, and the true value of whose property during the ten years between 1860 and 1870 was diminished to the amount of over two thousand millions of dollars, as shown by the census of the United States.

The indignation of the Southern whites against the spoliation to which they were thus subjected, by the aid of the administration and congressional majority, was further aroused by the federal office-holders, who, with their adherents and the support of their party at Washington, controlled elections, and tampered with the courts and usurped their power. Legislatures were seized, needless and obnoxious acts passed, and nothing was neglected to foster and perpetuate enmity and strife between the two races. A regard for the real interests of the colored men which could only be promoted by advancing his sense of political justice, in harmony with the interests of the whites, was no part of the schemes. The old proverbial game of oppressors, to divide the people against each other, so as to conquer and rob them all, was never more recklessly pursued than in the too successful efforts to set race against race, and the North and South against each other. The beneficial restoration of concord and the Union can only be effected by fair dealing and constitutional liberty.

Directly injurious as the impoverished and dishonestly taxed condition of the South is to the Northern people, its dangers are secondary in importance to the results which must follow to the people of the whole Union if the continuation of military interference and despotism, such as have been conspicuously exemplified in Georgia, Louisiana, and Arkansas, is permitted. All simply local and domestic matters must, under the constitution, be left to the people of the States. At last, the practices of the Republican party are echoed in the speeches of its leaders, who attempt to justify the progress of centralization—a system absolutely contrary to all free and especially to all really republican government.

The Political Color-line.

One of the first objects in the Democratic Southern policy should be to destroy the political "color-line," which it has been the constant aim of those who had no desire for the welfare either of the white or colored race to intensify to the utmost. If it should be perpetuated, and the colored people continue to be made the tools of those who maintain corrupt government, both at the South and North, the ultimate result will be especially disastrous to those who, in comparison with the rest of the population of the Union, are in a small minority. Their practical welfare can best be promoted by such a general prosperity of the South as will give them a fair day's wages for a fair day's work, and improve their education and sound intelligence on public affairs, so that by their own free and honest efforts they may earn the respect of all men, and, judging for themselves on political questions, may be independent of dictation by sordid and selfish intriguers. When the federal government ceases to interfere in the affairs of separate States, and is represented in the South by office-holders whose character will command respect and esteem, a complete and harmonious settlement of the political questions in those States will soon be attained. Attachment to the Union will be increased when an administration fulfills the duty of making union a blessing.

We find that in those States where the Democratic party has power, trade and credit have revived, enterprise has increased, and harmony between the races been promoted. It should be thoroughly understood that the freedom and enfranchisement of the colored man, as fixed in the constitution, are permanent and indisputable. A cardinal doctrine in the National Democratic platform might well be copied from that of the Democratic and conservative people of Mississippi in the words,

"We recognize and will maintain the civil and political equality of all men as established by the Constitution of the United States and the amendments thereto."

Popularity of Democratic Principles.

From the first organization of parties in the United States until the inauguration of President Lincoln, democratic principles have almost always commanded the approval of the people. They are the essential life of the Republic. When questions relative to slavery became paramount to all others, a new party of miscellaneous origin arose based on these alone. The nation being plunged into war, the anti-democratic portion of the Republican party took advantage of the passions and delusions incident to the occasion, and enforced its views of finance, revenue, and the administration of government. These have been carried far toward their logical results, as is seen in the disastrous condition of the country. The people are anxious for a return to the practice of sound principles. Of this they gave unmistakable evidence at the elections of 1873–4, when the opposition polled over three millions and a half of votes, a clear gain to them of over half a million, with a corresponding loss to the party of the administration.

Can the Republicans be Trusted ?

The Republican leaders, thus driven to the wall by an indignant people, are attempting to place themselves on Democratic platforms. Can they be trusted? Is the method of trusting old and persistent offenders to reform themselves, and retaining them in positions of the highest responsibility and confidence, after a long series of broken promises, one that commends itself to common sense, either in jurisprudence or any affairs of State or ordinary life? But we are not left to judge the party by the application of general principles. It is condemned by its own acts.

Three years ago, in the national platform of the Republicans, the party pledged itself to the enactment of laws which would "make honesty, efficiency, and fidelity the essential qualifications for office." But such exposures have throughout that period continued to be made as incalculably exceed those which at any former time would have irretrievably condemned any admininistration or party. They give us mere glimpses of the evils which leaven the whole system. The President and Congress alike abandoned and repudiated the effort to reform. In spite of frequent pledges of economy, the ordinary expenditures of the government in 1874 far exceeded those of any year since 1868, and Congress at its last session voted for $40,000,000 of additional taxes, a sum which alone is two thirds of the whole cost of the government of the United States in its last year under Democratic rule. Ten years ago, and repeatedly since that time, the party in power announced that a return to specie payments was one of its cardinal principles; and yet we are now further from it and the greenback is more depreciated than it was five years ago. The party has practically persevered in the fictions by which it imperiled the Union and impoverished the people. Nothing has been done to promote commerce, restore the American flag to its former proud position on the ocean, revive manufactures, or relieve all classes and replenish the treasury by means of a revenue tariff. The oppression of the South yet continues, although, in obedience to the distinct and unmistakable demand of the people of the North, its acts have become less glaring. But the desire of the administration for centralization and to keep itself in power by military and despotic measures remains unabated.

Conclusions.

On every point, the administration and leaders of the Republican party have amply proved that, however specious their promises may be, no confidence can be placed in them; while the people, by an overwhelming vote, and by a common impulse throughout the Union, have already shown their knowledge of the fact and recorded an emphatic verdict. All the well-meant efforts to form a new party have failed as signally as the attempts of honest Republicans to purify the organization to which they have belonged. Those defeats and the recent and signal victories of the Democratic party, aided by other independent and patriotic voters, establish the fact that it is the only strong and organized opposition to the abuses which oppress the people. Its principles, directly at variance with those errors and evils which have long predominated in the Republican party, make it necessarily the party of reform. The Republican party is held in hand by leaders who are linked together in various rings, and will practically, if secretly, combine to frustrate all sound and comprehensive effects of beneficial changes. Hence the only hope of restoring the nation to its former prosperity, and the government to purity, is by continuing to combine the power of the Democratic party with that of its new allies, who, by deserting it, would throw their weight against the reforms they justly desire.

The number of steadfast and reliable Democratic voters alone is over three millions. This is sufficient proof that they must form the nucleus of all successful opposition to the administration and its abuses, and that no third party of Reformers, split from the Republican, can have any reasonable hope of vitality within any independent organization. Thus the Presidential election in 1876 must be a straight contest between the Democrats and Republicans. Such a nomination as that which disheartened Democrats and resulted in failure must not be repeated. The platform must be liberal and sound. Thoroughly as business men and others appreciate the necessity of a change, much will depend on the selection of the candidates for the Presidency and Vice-Presidency. It is essential not only that they must both be Democrats, but also men of sterling and reliable character, both personally and politically. It will not be satisfactory to the vast series of States known as the North, unless both of them are from that part of the Union. This course also is that which will best insure pacification and prosperity in the South. The Democrats will cordially welcome all support of their principles, without inquiring out the partisan antecedents of those who offer it. If those conditions meet due compliance, we shall find that the "cohesive power of public plunder" is strong only when the thought and power of the people are dormant. It will vanish like a mist when honest men, duly aroused by a sense of the impending dangers, once more act together for the protection of themselves and their country.

www.ingramcontent.com/pod-product-compliance
Lightning Source LLC
LaVergne TN
LVHW011128110826
845150LV00008B/2273

9781418195250